SUPER SPORTS

Rock Climbing
and
Mountaineering

DAVID JEFFERIS

RAINTREE
STECK-VAUGHN
PUBLISHERS

A Harcourt Company

Austin   New York
www.raintreesteckvaughn.com

▲ Using a rope to go down a rock face is called rappelling.

Published by Raintree Steck-Vaughn Publishers, an imprint of Steck-Vaughn Company

Library of Congress Cataloging-in-Publication Data

Jefferis, David.
    Rock Climbing and Mountaineering / David Jefferis.
        p. cm. -- (Super sports)
    Includes bibliographical references (p.) and index.
    ISBN 0-7398-4346-X
        1. Mountaineering--Juvenile literature.
2. Mountains--Recreational use--Juvenile literature.
[1. Mountaineering. 2. Mountains--Recreational use.
3. Outdoor recreation.] I. Title. II. Super sports (Austin, Tex.)

GV200 .J44 2001
796.52'2--dc21   2001019203

Acknowledgments
We wish to thank the following individuals and organizations for their help and assistance and for supplying material in their collections:
Action-Plus Photographic, All Sport, All Sport USA, Alpha Archive, Steve Bardens, Mark Buscail, John Cleare, J. Corripio, Chris Craggs, David Davies, Bernard Giani, John Gichigi, M. Glaister, Nick Groves, Harry How, Tadashi Kajiyama, David Keaton, Duncan McCallum, Mountain Camera Picture Library, PGL Boreatton Park,
Mike Powell,
Ian Smith, J. Stock,
Stockshot, Pascal
Tournaire, Vandystadt
Photo Agency,
E. Williams

Diagrams by
Gavin Page

Printed in China and
bound in the United States.

1 2 3 4 5 6 7 05 04 03 02 01

Take care of yourself!
Mountains can be dangerous places. NEVER go for a walk without telling an adult where you are going. NEVER go climbing without an expert to tell you what to do.

Contents

World of Mountain Sports   4

Walk or Scramble?   6

Mountain Trails   8

Mountain Camp   10

Weather Watch   12

Rappelling   14

Starting Off   16

Bouldering   18

Ice and Snow   20

Roof of the World   22

New Ideas   24

Mountain Sport Facts   26

Mountain Sport Words   28

Mountain Science   30

Index   32

Look out for the Super Sports symbol

Look for the equipment symbol in boxes like this.
Here you will find extra mountain sport facts, stories,
and useful tips for beginners.

World of Mountain Sports

▲ After a hard climb to reach the top, this climber is able to take some time to look at the fantastic view!

Mountain sports are exciting. They require good equipment and lots of teamwork.

Mountain sports are not just about climbing up to the very top of a mountain. Many people like to walk, hike, or scramble up lower slopes for the fresh air and exercise.

Mountainous areas can be dangerous, so safety and survival skills are important on all trips.

▶ An expert and two beginners get ready for some climbing.

▲ Basic climbing skills are often taught at adventure camps.

◀ Climbers tackle steep cliffs and rocky slopes. They also cope with icy cold and bad weather.

▶ Many people enjoy the challenge of rock climbing.

Walk or Scramble?

Many people are eager to stay on marked paths when they go hill walking. Others like to leave the trail and scramble among the rocks.

▲ Anyone out on a hill or mountain has to plan for bad weather by taking suitable clothes and equipment.

A walk in the mountains takes planning. A hiking kit like the one below is a good idea. It's sensible to leave a note of the route and expected time of return.

Scrambling is more effort than walking, but not as hard as climbing. Scramblers use their hands to help pull themselves up slopes. A rope may be used for safety on difficult parts. It is much like mountaineering was in the early nineteenth century, when climbers had only simple equipment. They did it with warm clothes, tough boots, ropes, and a walking stick.

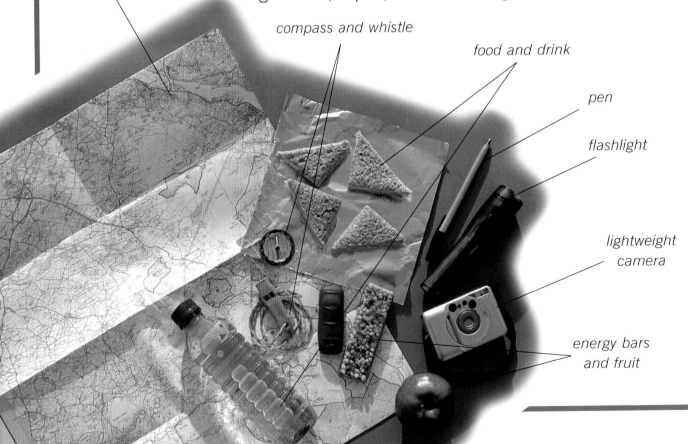

up-to-date map

compass and whistle

food and drink

pen

flashlight

lightweight camera

energy bars and fruit

▲ Protection from hot sun is very important. Walkers often wear a hat and protect their skin with sunblock cream.

◄ Even a short trip could include this equipment. Use the pen to mark a route on the map. You must be able to read the map well. Instead of the hand flashlight, you could try one you wear on your head. It is strapped around the forehead, keeping both hands free. Use a small camera to record highlights.

Caring for the environment

Hills and mountains are beautiful places. Keep them that way by remembering some easy tips:

√   Do close gates after you go through them, even if they were open when you went in.

√   Do stay away from wild animals. Most stay away, but some are dangerous if cornered.

√   Do put litter, cans, and bottles in a bag. An animal or another climber may get cut by the sharp edges.

√   Do bury food waste in the ground if it will rot. If in doubt, bag it up with other litter and take it home.

√   Don't pick wildflowers or plants.

√   Don't write or carve your name on rocks or trees, or leave graffiti anywhere.

Mountain Trails

Exploring high mountain trails is a good adventure sport for people who like to get away from crowded towns and cities.

▲ Water melted from mountain ice often forms blue-green lakes. This one is in the Canadian Rocky Mountains.

Many walkers and scramblers like to walk in remote places, far away from busy roads and towns.

Some countries make such hikes easy. For example, in Switzerland there is a system of well-kept hiking paths. These take walkers over hundreds of mountain passes and through grassy valleys.

▶ Climbers in Nepal look at some of the world's highest mountains.

◀ Early-morning sun lights mountain tops long before it reaches down into valleys.

Look out for mountain creatures

Many animals live in mountain country, but they usually keep away from humans.

Birds are quite easy to spot. They include eagles and vultures, that circle in the sky while looking down for food. You may also see mountain goats on tracks that are too steep and narrow for people.

Goats trot along mountain paths.

Birds use air currents to stay in flight.

Mountain Camp

The best camping gear is strong and light in weight. It should also be easy to use in awkward spots or in bad weather.

Picking a good campsite is important, even if it's only for one night. Experienced campers try to avoid places that will get soggy if it rains.

In high places, the main goal for a camper is to try to find a sheltered spot, with some protection from icy winds or heavy rain.

A modern lightweight tent is usually easy to put up, but it's always a good idea to practice at home first, to see how it works.

▲ In some countries, campers in forests hang food between trees, away from tents. Hungry animals are then less likely to come near the campsite.

 ## Remember to take a first-aid kit

Bad injuries are rare, but cuts and scrapes are common. It's always a good idea to carry a simple first-aid kit.

Items to take include bandages and cream for blisters or cuts and scrapes. Gauze and surgical tape are useful for bigger wounds. A pair of tweezers is good for removing splinters and thorns.

items stay clean in a small zip bag

◄ A camper cooks a meal using a small gas stove. The stove uses fuel from a screw-in cylinder. The campers sit on a plastic-foam sleeping mat so they do not get wet.

▼ A nylon tent gives shelter at night. This is a lightweight model that can be packed away easily for carrying.

The tent folds away into a small bag.

Weather Watch

Being prepared is the best way to stay safe in the mountains. Skilled climbers always check for changes in the weather.

▲ Bad weather may close in very quickly. So being aware of changes in the weather is important.

People who love the mountains usually become very good at reading the sky for signs of changing weather. It's not unusual for a storm to brew up in less than an hour. So hikers and climbers always need weatherproof clothes.

A whistle can be used to signal for help. The distress sign is six long blasts. It is repeated after a minute. At night, even a small flashlight may be a lifesaver if there are cliffs or steep drops nearby. To avoid getting lost, the hiker must carry up-to-date maps and a compass.

▲ Climbers lose a lot of water by sweating. So they need plenty of liquids to replace it.

A good supply of water is essential, especially in hot weather.

The wind-chill factor

Moving air cools your skin faster than still air, which is why a breeze on a hot day feels so good.

In cold weather, a wind makes us feel even colder, an effect called wind-chill. In icy weather, frostbite is a danger.

The best way to fight wind-chill is to wear windproof and waterproof clothing, with gloves to keep the fingers warm.

◀ Special gloves and clothing keep this climber warm in snow and ice.

Rappelling

Rappelling is a quick way to go down a steep cliff. Climbers use ropes to control the speed of descent.

Many adventure sports camps teach rappelling. These are good places to learn, as expert instructors are on hand to make sure that nothing goes wrong.

Rappelling is a way to get past a difficult overhang that has few hand or footholds. It is also a fast way to go down a rock face if the weather starts to change for the worse. But in all conditions, especially in bad weather, rappelling has to be done with great care.

◀ Here a beginner learns to rappell down a rock face. The ropes are clipped to a harness, worn around the waist and thighs.

The instructor makes sure the descent is carried out safely.

▲ It is important to wear safety helmets, even on easy practice rocks.

The first time is tough!

Rappelling off the edge of a rock face is a test of nerves. You stand on top of a rock face and lean backwards, trusting that the ropes won't break.

Then, you slowly edge out until your feet go over the edge. Finally, it is easy to walk down the slope.

Starting Off

Climbers can learn some basic skills in just a few days. The most important is getting the eyes, hands, and feet to work well together.

Climbing is more a matter of method and skill than great strength and muscle power. A climber starts off by standing back to see where the climb goes, and what rock features will make hand and foot holds on the way up.

Beginners soon learn to tie knots, use ropes, and clip these to a nylon harness. This spreads the pressure from a rope, making climbing easier and safer, especially in a fall.

▲ It's the first time up a rock face for this beginner. The instructor (top) holds the safety rope and points out the best hand and foot holds.

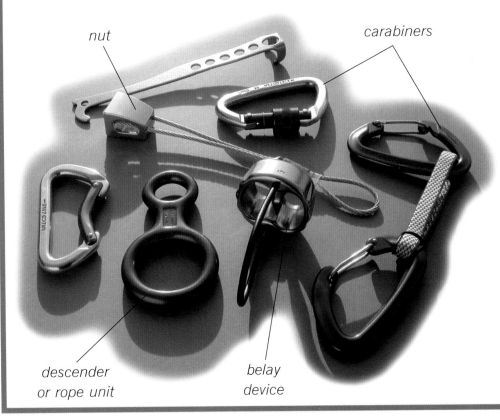

nut

carabiners

descender
or rope unit

belay
device

◀ Here are some tools used by rock climbers. A nut can be wedged in a crack to hold a rope. A carabiner is a metal clip that links a climber to a rope. Descenders and belay devices are used when rappelling. The belay device secures or stops the rope.

◄ Climbing walls are specially made for practice, but they may also be used for events. Here two climbers move up an artificial rock face built indoors.

safety rope fixed to climber in case of a fall

rope clipped to waist harness by carabiner

▶ This climber likes to practice in her spare time, so she has a small climbing wall fixed up in her bedroom.

Bouldering

Bouldering is the sport of climbing large rocks without using any equipment. It is a good way for climbers to practice their skills.

▲ This outcrop of rock is just right for climbing practice.

The great thing about bouldering is that a climber needs no safety equipment, because the idea is not to go any higher than it is safe to jump off.

Many climbers use boulders for fun and practice. They can work out climbing methods, such as a way to get up a rock face in a certain time, or climbing by various routes.

▶ This boulder was pushed into the valley by a glacier thousands of years ago. Today an expert climber practices on it. The top of the rock is too high for children though!

 Beware loose rocks!

Climbers soon learn that most rock faces have some loose or unsafe parts. There are easy ways to check if a handhold is safe, including rocking it back and forth to see if it will take your weight.

One climber in the Italian Alps who did not check a hold had a real surprise. A big chunk of cliff face broke free, and all he could do as he slid down was to push into the loose rock with his hands and feet. Luckily there was enough grip, and he was safe.

chalk soaks up sweat from hot hands

◀ Rock climbers may sprinkle chalk on their hands for grip.

Ice and Snow

An ice ax and spiked crampons are essential pieces of equipment for climbers who enjoy tackling snow-covered mountain peaks.

◀ A climber climbs a frozen wall, using an ice ax and crampons to move upwards.

The top of an ice ax is called the head. It has a sharp pick at one end and a flat spade, called an adze, at the other. The adze is useful for digging or cutting holds, while the pick can be used as a hook.

A crampon is a spiked frame fixed to a boot. Sharp spikes on the bottom and front give you a firm grip on ice.

Spikes in the crampons dig into the ice.

 Different kinds of snow

Snow is one of the most changeable things in nature. It ranges from a soft, dry powder to firm snow that may be almost as hard as ice.

Climbing through deep, soft snow is slow work, even for a team. The leader does most of the hard work, making either steps or a trench for the other climbers to use.

Experienced teams change the lead often, so no single climber does all the hard work.

▲ An avalanche is a mass of loose snow and ice that roars down the side of a mountain. Any climber who is in the way may be swept away or buried.

◀ A frozen waterfall looks like a difficult climb. In fact, on this one there are lots of hand and foot holds, and plenty of grip for the two ice axes.

Roof of the World

Most of the world's highest mountains are in the Himalayas. This huge range is in Asia, between India and China.

▲ Himalayan expeditions often make several camps on their way up to the summit of a mountain.

Climbing really high mountains is very different from day-to-day climbing. Above 8,202 feet (2500 m), most people become breathless and tired. The air is so thin that climbers may spend a week just getting used to it, before they can start to climb.

Bad weather may prevent a start for days, even weeks, since no expedition wants to be trapped on a mountain in a blizzard.

◀ Climbers are roped securely when rappelling between high peaks.

Mount Everest is the highest mountain in the Himalayas. Climbers first reached its 29,028 feet (8848 m) summit in 1953.

At this height the air is very thin, and almost all climbers who have tackled Everest have used a special air supply for breathing. The equipment is made up of a face mask, joined by rubber hose to a backpack air tank.

▲ Climbers make their way slowly towards the summit of Mount Everest.

New Ideas

Designers are always improving climbing equipment. Better materials lead to lighter, yet stronger gear. Satellite systems help with navigation.

▲ Cheap air travel makes it easier for people to go trekking in faraway places.

New equipment makes mountain sports easier. For example, the latest carabiners weigh far less than older steel types, but they are much stronger.

Modern clothing is better, too. Fabrics now keep a climber warm, yet allow body moisture to escape.

New mountain sports appear from time to time. Solo climbing is one of these. Here a climber tackles an ascent alone, without using high-tech equipment.

▼ A solo climber crosses a rock face.

 High-tech navigation

The GPS (global positioning system) computerized navigator can make life simpler for people in the mountains. GPS uses a system of satellites to work out an exact position, anywhere on Earth. This model is the size of a mobile phone and shows position, height, and direction. Even so, it is no replacement for old-fashioned skills with a map and compass!

This GPS screen shows height and position.

◀ One thing stays the same—the thrill of getting to the top!

Mountain Sport Facts

Here are some facts and stories from the world of mountain sports

▲ The first climbers to reach the summit of Mt. Everest were Edmund Hillary (left) and Tensing Norgay.

Highest mountain

The world's highest mountain is Mt. Everest. It lies on the borders of Tibet and Nepal.

Everest is 29,028 feet (8848 m) high, and was first climbed in 1953.

No oxygen

Most Everest climbers have taken an air supply because of the thin air. But in 1978 Reinhold Messner and Peter Habeler climbed the mountain without any air supplies at all.

Haunted heights

In the Middle Ages, many people thought mountains were haunted. In Germany people claimed to see ghostly figures near a peak in the Harz Mountains. In fact, the "ghosts" were shadows on misty clouds, cast by the sun at certain times of day!

First climbers

There was very little sport mountaineering before 1850. But between 1854 and 1865, many Alpine peaks were climbed for the first time. By 1900 climbers had tackled many of the highest mountains around the world.

◄ Mt. Blanc is the tallest mountain in the Alps, at 15,771 feet (4807 m) high. It was first climbed in 1786. Today there are lots of routes up to the top.

◀ Climbers make their way across a tangle of fallen ice. They are roped together for safety.

So you like heights?

Above 8,202 feet (2500 m) there are all kinds of health risks. Feeling dizzy and sick from a lack of oxygen in the air is common. A sore, bleeding nose may be caused from the dry air.

Wrecking the rocks

In the 1960s, many climbers used hard steel pegs to fix their lines. Many rock faces were chipped away by these pegs. People today mostly climb "clean," using tools that are kinder to the environment.

Fastest down Everest

Davo Karnicar took a month to climb Everest in 2000, but he came down in less than five hours. How? He was the first person to ski down!

Heavy to light...

A century ago, climbers usually wore thick clothes, and heavy, nailed boots. They carried a big wooden ax, called an alpenstock. As climbing became more popular, equipment improved. The alpenstock developed into the modern lightweight ice ax. Early crampons were first used in the 1800s.

Five days up a cliff

The world's highest sea cliff is the Thumbnail, in Greenland. It comes out of the sea, rising for 4,488 feet (1368 m). Four climbers tackled the cliff in 2000. It took them five days to reach the top, and they had to rent a dinghy to get to the start of the climb!

...and lighter still

The tiny pocket size camping stove is a climber's delight. It weighs just 3 oz (86 g), less than a small apple. When plugged in to a gas cylinder, it can boil a quart (l) of water in a few minutes.

◀ Mt. Everest is the highest mountain in the world. Lower down on its slopes are many glaciers.

Mountain Sport Words

▲ A carabiner holds a rope.

H ere are some technical terms used in this book.

alpenstock (AL-puhn-stock)
A type of wooden ax used by early climbers.

anchor (ANG-kur)
Point of attachment. It can be a natural anchor, such as a rock, or a tool, such as a nut.

avalanche (AV-uh-lanch)
A mass of snow or ice that breaks loose from a mountain, and comes down at high speed.

belay (bi-LAY)
To make the rope secure so that a fall is prevented.

blizzard (BLIZ-urd)
A violent storm with driving snow and wind.

bouldering (BOHL-dur-ing)
Climbing a large rock (or small cliff) without having to use a rope or other safety equipment. The idea is to go no higher up the boulder than where it is safe to jump off.

carabiner (kar-uh-BEE-nuhr)
An oval, or D-shaped metal-link with a spring or screw gate. Its main use is to join anchors to ropes.

climbing wall (KLIME-ing wawl)
Artificial wall, with molded hand and foot holds. Most walls are built indoors and are used for year-round training.

crampon (KRAM-pon)
A metal frame that can be attached to a climbing boot. Crampons have spikes that point down and forward. They are used to grip ice and hard snow.

face (fayss)
Any large area of rock, snow, or ice that is unbroken or that has few features sticking out.

frostbite (FRAWST-bite)
Damage to the body caused by icy chill. In extreme cold, blood may stop flowing to body parts such as fingers, toes, and ears. When this happens, the tissue dies, and the affected area may have to be removed.

gauze (gawz)
A piece of soft cotton, used to dress a wound.

◄ A climber looks for hand holds on a rock face.

◀ The Athabaska glacier flows in the Canadian Rocky Mountains. The bottom end of such a glacier is called the snout.

— *snout*

glacier (GLAY-shur)
A huge mass of ice that flows slowly down a mountain. The lower melting parts feed streams and rivers.

GPS
Short for Global Positioning System, a number of satellites that send radio signals down to the Earth. A GPS receiver picks up these signals and can record its position, anywhere on our planet.

harness (HAR-niss)
A piece of equipment that joins a climber to a rope, and spreads the load in a fall. It may be a sit-harness, which is worn around the waist and thighs, or a full-body harness.

hold (hohld)
Any part of rock or ice (such as a crack or outcrop) that can be used by the hands or feet for climbing. Also called a grip or handhold.

ice ax (eyess aks)
A tool used on snow and ice. It can be used for cutting, for digging, as an anchor, even for breaking a slide after a fall.

nut (nuht)
A metal tool which is wedged into a crack to hold a rope.

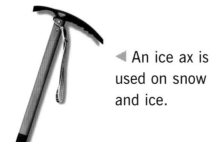

◀ An ice ax is used on snow and ice.

overhang (OH-vur-HANG)
Any part of a rock or cliff face that sticks out beyond the rest of the surface.

oxygen (OK-suh-juhn)
One of the gases in the air that is essential for all animals, including humans.

rappell (rap-PEL)
A method of coming down a rock face or overhang, using a rope and usually a harness.

solo climber
(SOH-loh KLIME-ur)
Someone who climbs alone and does not use ropes. Free climbers use a rope for safety but use natural holds.

sun-block cream
(SUHN-BLOK kreem)
Cream rubbed on to exposed skin to reduce sunburn.

windchill (wind-chil)
The effect of wind taking away heat from the body, so the skin feels colder than the surrounding air.

Mountain Science

There is a lot to learn about the world of mountains.

Cracking rocks

One of the ways that mountains get a jagged look is by splitting. This may happen when water seeps into a crack and then freezes. As the water turns to ice, it gets slightly bigger, so forcing the two sides of the rock slowly apart, and breaking them.

◄ These rocks split into jagged pieces as ice gets to work inside cracks just below the surface.

Ice expands

This experiment shows you an unusual fact about water. Unlike most materials that shrink as they get colder, water expands (gets bigger) when it turns to ice.

1 You need an empty yogurt cup, some water, a waterproof marker, and a freezer.

2 Mark a waterline clearly with the pen. Make this about 1/4 inch (5 mm) from the top of the pot.

Building mountains

Many mountains are formed when two parts of the Earth's surface push against each other. You can see the effect in this experiment. All you need are two sheets of plain paper.

China
Himalayas

◀ India and China are slowly pushing together, creating a mountain range called the Himalayas.

India

1 Fold the sheets carefully, to make them into zigzag mountain shapes. Lay them out on a flat surface, next to each other.

2 Push the sheets slowly towards each other. As you push, the touching edges of the sheets should rise up, like mountains.

waterline mark below top of ice

125g℮

3 Carefully fill the yogurt cup with water, up to the marked waterline.

4 Place the cup in the freezer compartment of a refrigerator. Leave overnight.

5 Next morning, you will see that the top of the ice is above the line you marked.

Index

alpenstock 27, 28
anchor 28, 29
animals, wild 7, 9, 10
avalanches 21, 28

belay 16, 28
blizzard 22, 28
bouldering 18, 19, 28

camping 10, 11
carabiner 16, 17, 24, 29
cliffs 5, 14, 27, 29
climbing wall 17, 28
clothing 6, 13, 24, 27
crampons 20, 27, 28

equipment 4, 6, 7, 18, 20,
    23, 24, 27, 28, 29

free climber 29
frostbite 13, 28

glaciers 18, 29
GPS navigator 25, 29

harness 14, 16, 17, 29
holds 14, 16, 21, 28, 29

ice 13, 20, 21, 27, 28, 29,
    30

ice ax 20, 21, 27, 29

maps 6, 7, 12, 25
mountains
    Blanc 26
    Brocken 26
    Everest 23, 26, 27
mountain climbers
    Habeler, Peter 26
    Hillary, Edmund 26
    Karnicar, Davo 26, 27
    Messner, Reinhold 26
    Norgay, Tensing 26
mountain ranges
    Alps 18, 26
    Canadian Rockies 8, 29
    Harz 26
    Himalayas 22, 23,
        26, 31
mountain science 30, 31
mountain trails 8

overhang 14, 28, 29
oxygen 27, 29

rappelling 2, 14, 15, 16,
    22, 28
rock face 2, 14, 15, 16, 18,
    24, 27, 28, 29
ropes 14, 15, 16, 17, 27, 28,
    29

safety 4, 16, 18
scrambling 4, 6, 8
snow 13, 20, 21, 28, 29
solo climber 24, 29
Switzerland 8

Thumbnail, Greenland 27
trekking 8, 24

walking 4, 6, 7, 8
weather 5, 6, 10, 12, 13,
    14, 22
windchill 13, 29